Original title:

Kaleidoscope Rays Above the Gnome Brook

Author: Johan Kirsipuu

ISBN HARDBACK: 978-1-80559-213-6

ISBN PAPERBACK: 978-1-80559-712-4

Whispers of Color in the Meadow

In morning light, the daisies sway,
A canvas bright, where colors play.
Breezes carry fragrant song,
Nature's dance, where hearts belong.

Butterflies with wings like flame,
In whispered hues, they call your name.
A symphony of softest grace,
In this meadow, find your place.

Reflections in a Prismatic Stream

Crystal waters, clear and bright,
Gather dreams in morning light.
Stones beneath, with tales to tell,
Where time slows, and wishes swell.

Ripples form a dance divine,
Every glance, a spark to shine.
Nature's mirror, secrets gleam,
In this flow, we chase a dream.

Dappled Light Over Enchanted Waters

Sunlight dances on the waves,
Creating magic that it saves.
Leaves above like whispers fall,
Casting shadows, a gentle call.

The water glimmers, stories blend,
Where every current seeks to mend.
A tapestry of light and shade,
In this haven, memories made.

The Spectrum of Dreams Beneath the Canopy

Underneath the leafy dome,
Where whispered dreams find their home.
Each color, bold, a tale unfolds,
In the silence, secrets told.

Shadows blend in twilight's hue,
A space where hopes and wishes grew.
Daring dreams take flight above,
Awash in warmth, an endless love.

Vivid Rhapsody Beneath the Sunset Canopy

Golden hues dance in the sky,
Whispers of twilight draw nigh.
Crimson clouds drift and sway,
Night's embrace bids day away.

Fingers of light intertwine,
Painting the world, so divine.
Shadows stretch, dreams appear,
In this moment, all is clear.

Branches frame the fading glow,
Where secrets of the sunset flow.
A symphony of colors blend,
Nature's canvas knows no end.

As stars awaken, one by one,
The serenade of night's begun.
With every heartbeat, time stands still,
In vivid rhapsody, hearts will fill.

The Embrace of Radiant Reflections

Mirrors of the lake so bright,
Holding whispers of soft light.
Gentle ripples kiss the shore,
In their dance, I long for more.

Each glance reveals a story told,
In silver tones, both brave and bold.
Nature's palette, rich and deep,
Awakening dreams from slumbered sleep.

Through the trees, sunlight spills,
Chasing doubts and quiet chills.
In the embrace, I find my peace,
Where every worry finds release.

Crystal beams of hope ignite,
As dawn breaks into light.
With radiant reflections near,
I find solace, pure and clear.

Whimsy in the Light-Dappled Woods

Under canopies green and bright,
Where fairies giggle, taking flight.
Dappled light dances on the ground,
In this haven, joy is found.

Mushrooms sprout in playful cheer,
Whispers of laughter fill the air.
Nature's wonders all around,
In the woods, delight is crowned.

A spiral dance of leaves above,
Gently cradles dreams and love.
Hidden paths twist, turn, and weave,
Calling forth those who believe.

Shadows play in the afternoon,
Accompanied by a sweet tune.
With whimsy as my guiding muse,
In this magic, I shall lose.

Elysian Colors of the Tranquil Brook

Whispers ripple through the stream,
In the sunlight, soft and gleam.
Colors swirl like a painter's brush,
Creating visions that gently hush.

Lilies float with grace and ease,
Kissed by the summer breeze.
Each stone tells a tale of time,
Nature's rhythm, pure and prime.

Butterflies flit from bloom to bloom,
In the heart of this sweet room.
Birds serenade with tender song,
In this place where I belong.

As evening falls, the colors blend,
A vivid journey without end.
In the tranquil brook's embrace,
I find my heart, my sacred space.

Sonata of Shades in a Lush Retreat

Beneath the leafy canopy,
Whispers dance on gentle air,
Colors blend in harmony,
Nature's breath, a tender care.

Sunlight filters through the trees,
Shadows play on forest floor,
Echoes sing with rustling leaves,
A symphony forevermore.

Mossy stones in quiet nooks,
Birds compose their tranquil song,
Every petal, every brook,
In the shade, where dreams belong.

Time flows slow, as moments weave,
Laughter mingles with the breeze,
In this realm, we're free to believe,
Nature's art, a heart that sees.

So let us linger, hand in hand,
In this lush, embracing space,
Together here, we understand,
In each shade, there's warm grace.

Field of Radiance by the Sparkling Brook

Golden hues embrace the morn,
Wildflowers sway in pure delight,
By the brook, a song is born,
Nature beams in soft sunlight.

Crickets hum, a cheerful tune,
Butterflies in joyful flight,
Underneath the gentle moon,
Twinkling stars adorn the night.

Streams of silver, quick and bright,
Whispers rush on pebbled ground,
In the field, life feels just right,
Harmony in every sound.

Youthful laughter fills the air,
Wind and water play their part,
Moments woven with such care,
Joyful echoes touch the heart.

In this space where spirits glide,
Freedom calls with every wave,
As the radiant blooms abide,
Nature's gift, forever brave.

The Lightplay Above an Enchanted Hollow

In the hollow, whispers flow,
Sunbeams dance with gentle grace,
Magic stirs in golden glow,
Secrets hide in this sweet place.

Echoes ring, like distant chimes,
Butterflies flit to and fro,
Nature sings in playful rhymes,
In this haven, time is slow.

Mossy beds and crystal streams,
Glowing orbs blink in delight,
Painting all our quiet dreams,
As day surrenders to night.

Stars awaken, brightly spun,
Casting spells from far above,
In this realm, we become one,
Wrapped in shadows, blessed by love.

So we linger, hearts entwined,
In the hollow's warm embrace,
Lost in light, forever blind,
To the world, we've found our place.

A Ray of Color in the Green Haven

In the haven, colors bloom,
Emerald leaves, a vibrant sea,
Fragrant petals gently loom,
Nature's brush, a masterpiece.

Every corner filled with life,
Sunlit patches kiss the ground,
Whispers soft, like sweetened strife,
In this garden, peace is found.

Dancing shadows, playful light,
Bees are humming, day's delight,
Amidst blooms, what a sight,
Harmony in nature's rite.

Let us wander, hand in hand,
Through this weave of green and gold,
In this place, our dreams expand,
Moments cherished, tales retold.

A ray of color, pure and bright,
In the haven, joy takes flight,
Nature's song, a soft invite,
Together here, our hearts ignite.

Mystical Shards of Beauty in Twilight's Gaze

In twilight's glow, the shadows dance,
Colors bleed in a fleeting trance.
Stars awaken, softly they gleam,
Whispers of beauty weave through a dream.

Winds carry secrets, tales untold,
As night enfolds, the world turns bold.
Moonlight kisses the silken streams,
Crafting magic from our hopes and dreams.

Petals unfurl, kissed by the night,
In fragrant blooms, there's pure delight.
Each moment captured, a fleeting breath,
Nature's canvas, a dance with death.

Auroras shimmer, light takes flight,
Whispers of dawn, breaking the night.
Mystical shards, in silence they rise,
Twilight's embrace, the heart complies.

Harmonies of Nature in Shaded Pools

Beneath the boughs, the waters sing,
Ripples echo with every fling.
Leaves murmur softly, secrets unfold,
In shaded pools, where time is gold.

The breeze brings melodies, sweet and clear,
Nature's chorus, a song we hear.
Birds harmonizing, soaring high,
In tranquil waters, the dreams reply.

Sunlight dapples, a gentle kiss,
Each ray a note in nature's bliss.
Ducklings paddle, laughter in streams,
Shaded pools cradle our wildest dreams.

Colors blend in a vibrant swirl,
Life a canvas, in motion it twirls.
Harmony flows, a rhythmic embrace,
In nature's heart, we find our place.

Elysian Blends on the Edge of Reality

On the cusp where dreams take flight,
Elysian blends weave day to night.
Clouds whisper secrets in softest hues,
Painting the sky with ethereal views.

Time dances gently, no rush to cease,
In this realm, we find our peace.
Colors mingle, a symphonic plight,
Reality bends in the fading light.

With every heartbeat, we drift away,
Into the magic where shadows play.
Thoughts intertwine like vines on stone,
In this space, we are never alone.

Celestial wonders, a radiant trail,
Guiding the lost, where hopes prevail.
Elysian dreams, an endless spree,
On reality's edge, we wander free.

Sunkissed Mosaics Along the Quiet Path

Gentle whispers along the way,
Sunkissed mosaics greet the day.
Each step a dance on golden ground,
In quiet paths, our hearts are found.

Wildflowers bloom in vibrant cheer,
Nature's palette, so brightly clear.
Sunlight dapples the forest floor,
In quiet moments, we seek for more.

Birdsong echoes through the trees,
A symphony carried by the breeze.
As shadows stretch, the world takes pause,
In this beauty, we find our cause.

Mosaics shimmer in the soft glow,
Paths intertwine where gentle winds flow.
Sunkissed journeys, souls intertwine,
Along the quiet path, you are mine.

Rays of Imagination in the Wildflower Meadow

Golden blooms in morning light,
Whispers dance, taking flight.
Colors blend, a vivid sway,
Dreams awaken in the fray.

Breezes carry tales untold,
Secrets of the earth unfold.
With each petal, stories spin,
Nature's heart beats deep within.

Crisp and fresh, the air invites,
Dancing shadows, golden sights.
Here, the soul finds its array,
In the wildflower's sweet ballet.

Moments caught in soft embrace,
Time slows down, a sacred space.
Thoughts bloom wide, horizons free,
In this meadow's reverie.

Rays of gold, a warm caress,
Filling hearts with pure finesse.
Every breath a gift that's dear,
In this place, there's naught to fear.

The Soft Glow at the Water's Bay

Silver ripples kiss the shore,
Whispers of the tide implore.
Stars reflect in twilight's grace,
Nature's mirror, a tranquil face.

Cool winds weave through gentle trees,
Lulling hearts with teasing breeze.
Moonlit paths of crystal gleam,
Carried forth with every dream.

Cranes stand tall, a graceful sight,
Underneath the fading light.
Their calls echo serenely clear,
In this bay, all feels so near.

Soft horizons, painted skies,
Embrace the night with lullabies.
Each wave murmurs cherished tales,
As time drifts on like whispered sails.

Underneath the starlit dome,
Hearts unite and find their home.
In this bay, love's gentle sway,
Guiding hopes till break of day.

A Mosaic Woven with Botanical Whispers

Petals bright, a grand display,
A mosaic where blooms play.
Nature's quilt of vibrant hues,
Stories wrapped in morning dew.

Leaves like whispers gently sigh,
Underneath the painted sky.
Colors dance, a rich refrain,
In this garden's sweet domain.

Bees hum softly, weaving truth,
In every blossom lies their proof.
Tendrils reach with patient grace,
Crafting beauty in this space.

Ferns unfurl, their secrets bare,
In this haven, love and care.
Touch and feel, let senses flow,
In the whispers of the grow.

A tapestry of life unfolds,
Harmonies through petals told.
In this garden, souls ignite,
With botanical flight in sight.

The Ethereal Light Over the Gnome Glen

In a glen where shadows play,
Ethereal lights guide the way.
Mushrooms glow in ghostly white,
Casting dreams into the night.

Gnomes at work, with laughter bright,
Fill the air with pure delight.
Tiny hands in concert weave,
Magic threads they soon believe.

Crickets sing, a soft refrain,
As the stars align in vein.
Each flicker sparkles in the dark,
An ancient realm begins to spark.

Bubbly streams and willow trees,
Swaying gently with the breeze.
Delicate whispers in the air,
Life awakens, rich and rare.

Gathered dreams in every nook,
In this glen, lost souls can look.
Ethereal light, gentle glow,
In its warmth, all hearts can know.

A Tapestry of Shadows and Glimmers

In twilight's grasp, the shadows play,
Whispers of dreams in colors sway.
A dance of light, both dark and bright,
Weaving the night with stars in sight.

Beneath the trees, the secrets unfold,
Stories of time in silence told.
A tapestry rich, with threads so fine,
Crafted by fate, a design divine.

As moonbeams stretch across the land,
Softly they touch, as if they'd planned.
The glimmers rise, like fireflies wing,
Nature's embrace, a gentle spring.

In shadows cast by glowing light,
Mysteries dance, both bold and slight.
A heart beats wild, where echoes roam,
In this realm, we find our home.

So let us wander, hand in hand,
Through winding paths of this enchanted land.
Where shadows blend with glimmers bright,
And silence sings of love's delight.

The Dancing Spectrum of Sylvan Serenity

Amidst the boughs where whispers weave,
A spectrum unfurls for hearts to believe.
Colors collide in the softest light,
Painting the day, embracing the night.

The leaves are canvases, bold and bright,
Where sunbeams dance with pure delight.
A gentle breeze carries the sound,
Of nature's song, where peace is found.

In sylvan realms, the spirit soars,
Through emerald halls and ancient doors.
Cascading hues in a sweet ballet,
A serenade to greet the day.

With every rustle, there's magic near,
A symphony played both soft and clear.
In this embrace, we lose our breath,
Finding in nature, the essence of depth.

Let us be still, let us be free,
In the dance of colors, in harmony.
For in these woods, our souls align,
In the spectrum's glow, forever entwined.

Fractals of Light Upon the Forest Floor

Amid the ferns, a fractal glow,
Patterns emerge in the earth's tableau.
Sunlight trickles through a leafy dome,
Illuminating pathways to roam.

Each step reveals a new design,
Nature's brushstrokes, a work divine.
As shadows play on mossy beds,
Stories of life through silence spreads.

The forest breathes with every sigh,
Infinite worlds beneath the sky.
Dappled light in rhythmic grace,
Whispers of time in this sacred space.

Fractals spin, a wondrous art,
Capturing magic, igniting the heart.
With every glance, a tale retold,
Of secrets hidden, of wonders bold.

Let us wander where the wild things dream,
In the fractals' dance, we find our theme.
Beneath the trees, forevermore,
Light and shadow on the forest floor.

Luminescent Dreams by the Burbling Brook

By the burbling brook, where shadows play,
Luminescent dreams weave night and day.
The water's song, soft and sweet,
Invites our hearts to skip a beat.

Glimpses of light on the rippling tide,
Where hopes and wishes come alive.
A symphony swirls in the evening mist,
Casting a spell not to be missed.

In this embrace of twilight's grace,
We find our peace, a sacred space.
Each drop of water, a wish held near,
A whisper of love that we long to hear.

As stars emerge, shyly they gleam,
Reflecting upon our luminescent dream.
With every ripple, new stories unfold,
In the brook's embrace, our spirits are bold.

So let us gather by the water's edge,
Where dreams are born, and hearts pledge.
In the glow of night, by the brook's soft flow,
Our souls entwined, forever to grow.

The Hidden Spectrum Underneath the Leaves

Whispers dance in the gentle breeze,
Colors woven through ancient trees.
A tapestry hidden from wandering eyes,
Secrets bloom where the silence lies.

Soft shadows play with the sun's warm touch,
Emerald glimmers beneath the crutch.
Rustling whispers tell tales of old,
Nature's palette, a story untold.

Every leaf a brushstroke divine,
In the quiet, their hues intertwine.
Glimmers of gold frame the verdant green,
A magic world, too rare to be seen.

Beneath the bark and within the ground,
Lies a spectrum of life, profound.
Each layer a note in the symphony,
Of colors unseen, yet felt deeply.

Celebrate the colors that softly speak,
In hidden realms where the heart can seek.
For beneath the leaves, life finds its way,
In the silent chorus of night and day.

Songs of Light in the Enchanted Hollow

In the heart of the wood, where the shadows lie,
A melody plays as the leaves flutter by.
Sunbeams filter through branches high,
Dancing with grace, like notes in the sky.

Bubbles of laughter from streams that roam,
Whispering secrets that feel like home.
Fireflies twinkle in rhythmic parade,
Casting soft glimmers that never fade.

Nature's symphony, a vibrant song,
Echoes through spaces where dreams belong.
Each rustle and croon, a heartbeat's embrace,
Where every corner holds magic's trace.

Hush now and listen, the world softly sighs,
As day turns to dusk and the night complies.
The tapestry woven with light and with song,
In the enchanted hollow, where soul feels strong.

With every breath, let the music flow,
Through vibrant colors that subtly glow.
In this sanctuary of calm and delight,
The songs of light paint the deepening night.

The Fractured Prism of Nature's Art

Crack the shell of the ordinary view,
And see the palette in every hue.
Nature's artistry in every shard,
A fractured prism, a life unbarred.

Through tangled branches, colors burst,
In vibrant shades that richly thirst.
The sky, a canvas of swirling bright,
Reflects the wonder of day and night.

Petals open in a tender display,
While shadows weave through the breaking day.
Every droplet glistens with tales to impart,
A masterpiece painted by nature's heart.

In the quiet moments, let your eyes feast,\nOn the chaotic
beauty, the wild at least.
For in every fracture, glimmers reside,
A truth of existence that cannot hide.

Celebrate the beauty that colors entwine,
In the fractured prism, where stars align.
For nature's art is forever free,
A vivid reminder of life's tapestry.

Tranquil Blues and Joyful Reds

In the tranquil hush of the dawning light,
Cerulean skies whisper, soft and bright.
The blues of the morning, calm and true,
Wrap the world in a vibrant view.

Joyful reds burst forth with a playful cheer,
Painting the horizon, drawing us near.
Strawberries sweet, and sunsets bold,
Moments of warmth in shades untold.

Waves lap softly on the sandy shore,
Where blues and reds mingle forevermore.
A dance of colors in every tide,
Nature's heartbeat, our guide and pride.

Wrap your heart in this delicate lace,
Feel the energy, embrace the grace.
Tranquil blues and joyful reds unite,
In a canvas of life, pure and bright.

Let the colors carry you away,
To a world where dreams find their play.
With every hue, let your spirit soar,
In the beauty of life, forever explore.

Fragments of Light Dancing Over Pebbles

Beneath the brook, the sunlight plays,
Shimmering rays in endless displays.
Pebbles glisten, a jeweled show,
Rippling waters in soft flow.

Whispers of dawn, the world awakes,
Nature's canvas, a dance it makes.
Tiny sparkles in gentle grace,
Every corner, a bright embrace.

Crystals scatter in shifting streams,
A symphony of luminous dreams.
With each ripple, reflections gleam,
Weaving magic, like a dream.

From shadowed depths, to sunlight's kiss,
Every pebble, a moment of bliss.
In this ballet, the earth rejoices,
Echoing nature's softest voices.

The Light's Embrace in a Secret Glade

In hidden realms where shadows linger,
Light weaves magic, soft as a finger.
Ferns sway lightly, kissed by the sun,
A secret glade where dreams are spun.

Golden beams pierce through emerald leaves,
Nature's whisper, a tale it weaves.
Gentle breezes, a caress divine,
In this sanctuary, the stars align.

Every bloom seems to dance alive,
In this haven, spirits thrive.
With every ray, a promise glows,
In every heart, the tranquility flows.

Beneath the boughs, a soft embrace,
Time stands still in this cherished place.
Harmony sings in the light's caress,
A tranquil world, forever blessed.

A Medley of Hues Amongst the Foliage

Crimson leaves, like flames of fall,
Gold and orange, nature's call.
Amidst the green, a vibrant show,
A tapestry where colors flow.

Each petal whispers in soft tones,
Echoes of beauty in nature's own.
At every turn, a painter's dream,
In the woods, life's vivid theme.

Twirling vines in graceful dance,
Sunlight dapples, a fleeting glance.
Colors merge in a glorious blend,
The foliage sings, as seasons send.

Textures woven, an artist's art,
Every shade plays its part.
In the heart of the forest, joy abounds,
In each lovely hue, true peace surrounds.

Celestial Sights in Gnome-filled Glens

Gnomes gather under twilight skies,
Stars awaken, the night's surprise.
In secret glens, their laughter bright,
Creating magic in the fading light.

Amidst the trees, a gentle gleam,
Moonlight dances, a silver dream.
Nature sighs in whispered tones,
Echoing truths in ancient stones.

Twinkling orbs in the midnight air,
A celestial ballet, nothing compares.
Guided by starlight, they dance and play,
In the stillness of night, they find their way.

Each glen a wonder, with stories untold,
Woven in stardust, aged but bold.
With heart and whimsy, they roam and share,
In this realm of enchantment, magic is rare.

Enchanted Colors of the Forgotten Vale

In a vale where whispers sing,
Vivid hues of springtime cling.
Petals dance in morning dew,
A tapestry of every hue.

Ancient trees with arms outstretched,
Colors bright and truly etched.
Birds that paint the skies with songs,
This magic place where heart belongs.

Sunlight filters through the leaves,
Color swirls where magic weaves.
Every shade, a tale to tell,
In the vale, all sorrows quell.

Rains of gold and violets' grace,
Add to nature's soft embrace.
Footsteps light on grassy knoll,
To the vale, it calls our soul.

As twilight drapes its velvet cloak,
The colors whisper, softly spoke.
In this enchanting place so clear,
The heart finds home, the spirit near.

Prismatic Dreams over Gentle Waters

Underneath the starlit skies,
Dreams arise in vibrant ties.
Reflections dance on water's face,
A world transformed in time and space.

Ripples weave a story bright,
Every wave, a splash of light.
Colors twist in calm embrace,
Prismatic tales that time can trace.

Moonlit paths of silver glow,
In the night, the colors flow.
Gentle breezes kiss the shore,
Echoes linger, wanting more.

Painted realms in dreams we sail,
Over water, soft and pale.
With every breath, the colors sigh,
Underneath the endless sky.

In this world of sweet delight,
Where dreams are born, and hearts take flight.
Subtle hues, a whispered song,
In the waters, we belong.

The Murmurs of a Chromatic Haven

Nestled deep where shadows play,
Colors sing at close of day.
Echoes dance on twilight's breath,
In this haven, life and death.

Leaves of jade and petals bright,
Whispers weave through day and night.
Every sound, a color's hue,
In this place where dreams come true.

A mosaic of the heart's delight,
In the haven, shadows ignite.
Colors merge in secrets shared,
With every moment, love declared.

Mysteries in twilight's song,
In this haven, we belong.
Fingers trace the vibrant air,
Marking each time, tender care.

As dawn unveils with golden thread,
In the haven, color spread.
Fading light on colors blend,
A place where every journey ends.

Magic in the Multicolored Glade

In a glade where wonders reign,
Colors radiant, free from pain.
Softly hums the gentle breeze,
Every shade a sweet reprise.

Dappled light through leafy green,
From the world, a tranquil sheen.
Lavender skies and golden beams,
Crafted softly from our dreams.

Fluttering wings and laughter bright,
In the glade, all feels right.
Colors swirl in joyful play,
As the sun begins to sway.

Magic whispers in the trees,
Tales of love upon the breeze.
Every corner filled with cheer,
In the glade, our path is clear.

As twilight paints the edges wide,
Colorful hues will not hide.
In this glade, our spirits soar,
Forever seeking, evermore.

The Glow of the Wandering Stream

In the twilight's gentle sway,
A stream meanders, soft and gray.
Its whispers dance through silent trees,
Carrying tales upon the breeze.

Beneath the stars, the waters gleam,
Reflecting dreams, a silver beam.
It sings of journeys far and wide,
Where secrets in its depths abide.

With each ripple, stories flow,
Of love and loss, of joy and woe.
In the moonlight, shadows play,
Along the banks where night holds sway.

The glow enchants the fading light,
As fireflies flit, a glowing sight.
The wandering stream knows every heart,
And carries whispers, a work of art.

So linger here, feel nature's might,
In the glow of the wandering night.
Let the stream's song guide your way,
In this magical end of day.

Glimmering Tales Told by Moonlight

Under a shroud of silver glow,
The world awakens, soft and slow.
Moonlight paints the fields so bright,
Telling tales in the still of night.

Whispers of ancients, secrets unfold,
In the quiet, their stories told.
Each beam of light a sacred thread,
Binding the living with the dead.

Crickets serenade with gentle sound,
As shadows weave in the mossy ground.
Together they dance, a tranquil ballet,
In the moon's embrace, they sway and play.

A path of shimmer leads us afar,
Where dreams take flight, and wishes star.
Glimmering tales in silver's embrace,
Draw us together, a timeless grace.

So let the moonlight guide your heart,
As stories glimmer, and shadows part.
In the night, we find our way,
With tales of wonder that softly sway.

Colorful Whispers in the Leafy Bower

In a nook where shadows fall,
Colorful whispers gently call.
Leaves flutter with stories unspun,
As sunlight dances, warm and fun.

Petals brush against the breeze,
Singing secrets from the trees.
The bower's charm, a vivid hue,
Wraps the world in wonder anew.

Fluttering wings of butterflies,
Painting the air beneath the skies.
Nature's canvas brings forth delight,
As moments blend, both soft and bright.

In every rustle, a tale is shared,
Of hopes and dreams, of hearts that dared.
Colorful whispers weave through the day,
In the leafy bower, weaving play.

So linger awhile, let the colors sing,
In the heart of nature, joy takes wing.
For in this space, so lush and free,
We find our place, in harmony.

Enchanted Glow of the Brookside Groves

Amidst the grove where willows sway,
The brookside glimmers, night and day.
With every ripple, magic stirs,
Each drop, a wish, as the night blurs.

The moonlight dances on water's face,
Embracing the night in a warm embrace.
Whispers of dreams ride the gentle flow,
In the enchanted glow, hearts do grow.

Branches arch, a leafy veil,
Hiding secrets, a poignant tale.
The brook sings soft, a lullaby,
As stars twinkle in the midnight sky.

Fairies flit beneath the boughs,
Beneath the watchful, ancient vows.
The glowing brookside calls us near,
A haven found, devoid of fear.

So wander here, let spirits soar,
In the glow of groves, forevermore.
For in this place, all wonders gleam,
In the enchanted glow, we dream.

The Easel of Nature's Imagination

In the meadow, colors blend,
Brush strokes dance with every wind.
Flowers whisper, leaves engage,
Nature's beauty on life's stage.

Mountains rise with hues so bold,
Their silent stories yet untold.
Clouds like canvases drift by,
Painting dreams across the sky.

Rivers flow, a vivid stream,
Reflecting sunlight, a golden gleam.
Sunset's palette paints the night,
Stars emerge to share their light.

Fields of gold in morning's bliss,
Each dawn a symphony, a kiss.
Nature's easel, grand and wide,
In her arms, we all abide.

With every season's gentle touch,
Art takes form beneath the brush.
Nature's heart beats, pure and free,
In this world, we're meant to be.

Echoes of Color in the Forest Air

In the forest, whispers sing,
Every leaf a vibrant thing.
Sunlight filters, shadows play,
Colors dance throughout the day.

Crimson berries, emerald ferns,
Nature's canvas, beauty turns.
Rustling branches share the tale,
Of life embraced in rich detail.

Golden rays through branches thread,
Gentle winds, a soft spread.
Echoes of color, pure delight,
Kissed by morning's softest light.

Mushrooms sprout in hues of blue,
Nature paints with every hue.
A spectrum found within the trees,
In the forest, hearts find ease.

Each step taken, art unfolds,
Through the leaves, a story told.
Echoes linger, colors rare,
In the forest's fragrant air.

Luminous Secrets Beneath the Arboreal Roof

Underneath the leafy arch,
Secrets hidden, nature's march.
Shimmering lights in gentle sway,
Guide the wanderers on their way.

Flickering fireflies, soft and bright,
Illuminate the velvet night.
Whispers softly touch the ground,
In this realm, magic is found.

Roots like veins, they twist and weave,
Tales of life we can't believe.
Luminous paths where shadows dance,
Invite the heart to take a chance.

Moss-clad stones in silence glow,
Telling stories of long ago.
Among the trunks, the spirits play,
Echoing dreams till break of day.

Beneath the trees, the world is deep,
Where ancient wisdom seems to seep.
In this haven, secrets thrive,
In nature's heart, we come alive.

Whirls of Color in Celestial Waters

In the lake, reflections spin,
Vibrant hues as day begins.
Ripples shimmer, colors whirl,
Nature's canvas starts to twirl.

Azure waves and golden light,
Dancing serenely, pure delight.
Winds caress the surface clear,
Whispers of beauty draw us near.

Petals float on sapphire tides,
Nature's treasures where joy abides.
Shadows play as dusk descends,
With each moment, magic blends.

Beneath the sky, horizons sing,
Every drop can feel a wing.
In the silence, colors gleam,
In celestial waters, we dream.

As twilight paints a canvas wide,
With blessings from the evening tide.
Whirls of color, soft as sighs,
Invite the heart to touch the skies.

A Symphony of Shades by the Water's Edge

The sun dips low, a golden hue,
Whispers of ripples play anew.
Colors dance in the setting light,
A canvas bright, a pure delight.

The sky reflects in liquid glass,
Where gentle winds of evening pass.
Shades of orange, pink, and blue,
Blend together in a joyful view.

Beneath the trees, shadows sway,
Nature conducts its soft ballet.
Each note sung by the rustling leaves,
A symphony the heart believes.

In perfect harmony, they call,
A serenade embracing all.
The water's edge, a sacred space,
Where every shade finds its place.

As night descends, the colors fade,
Yet in memory, they're never laid.
The whispers linger, soft and near,
A symphony we hold most dear.

The Enigma of Colorful Shadows

In twilight's glow, the shadows play,
Mysteries wrapped in shades of gray.
Each hue a tale that softly drapes,
The world adorned in brilliant shapes.

Colors whisper secrets untold,
In vibrant forms that capture bold.
The enigma hides just out of sight,
Waiting to reveal its light.

Through rustling leaves, the secrets glide,
Shadows dance with the evening tide.
A fleeting moment, captured fast,
Forgotten dreams from ages past.

With every step, a story spun,
In paled moonlight, all is one.
The chase of color draws us near,
Unraveling what we hold dear.

Through vibrant trails of thought we roam,
In colorful shadows, we find home.
The enigma calls, we walk the line,
In every shadow, colors shine.

Murmuring Streams and Radiant Dreams

In valleys deep where rivers sigh,
Murmurs echo, softly fly.
The liquid song, a soothing sound,
In nature's voice, our peace is found.

Beneath the boughs, dreams start to weave,
Radiant tales that never leave.
Each gentle wave and soothing stream,
Carries hopes upon its beam.

The sunlit dance on waters bright,
Awakens hearts in morning light.
As dreams cascaded down the shore,
A whispering promise to explore.

With every step near streams we tread,
The vibrant visions fill our head.
Nature's rhythm brings us peace,
In murmuring streams, our troubles cease.

So let us follow where they lead,
The winding paths through verdant seed.
For in their flow, our spirits soar,
Murmuring streams forevermore.

Ode to the Vivid Tranquility

In quietude where colors bloom,
An ode is sung, dispelling gloom.
Vivid hues, they blend and twirl,
In tranquil waves, we gently swirl.

The fields of green, the skies of blue,
A tapestry of nature's view.
Whispers breeze through emerald blades,
Where peace resides, and calm invades.

Soft petals fall from branches high,
A silent dance beneath the sky.
In every hue, a tale retold,
Of vibrant lives that never fold.

Serenity wrapped in colors bright,
An inner glow, a pure delight.
Each moment felt is deeply known,
In vivid tranquility we've grown.

Let every shade inspire the soul,
A harmony that makes us whole.
In nature's arms, we find our way,
An ode to peace, forever stay.

Nature's Palette Across the Faerie Glade

In the heart where soft winds sigh,
Colors dance in the azure sky.
Petals whisper secrets old,
Stories in their hues unfold.

Golden rays through branches slide,
Meadow blooms with gentle pride.
Crickets serenade the night,
As fireflies twinkle, pure delight.

Streams glisten like liquid glass,
Where curious creatures quietly pass.
Nature's art, a vivid spree,
In every leaf, a memory.

Beneath the shade of ancient trees,
The world hums with soft melodies.
Every shadow, every light,
Crafts a canvas full and bright.

In this glade, hearts intertwine,
Life's essence, a gift divine.
As twilight wraps the earth in glow,
Nature's palette, forever grows.

Glimmers of Wonder in the Whispering Pines

Beneath tall pines so proud and wise,
Where sunlight weaves through open skies.
A symphony in rustling leaves,
Nature whispers what the heart believes.

Shadows dance upon the ground,
Echoes of the softest sound.
With every breath, a story told,
Of dreams and wishes, brave and bold.

Mossy carpets underfoot,
Ancient roots, a soothing root.
Gentle breezes carry scents,
From blooming flowers, sweet suspense.

Nightfall comes with stars aglow,
In the stillness, wonders flow.
Moonlight splashes on the pine,
A magic realm, truly divine.

In whispers clear, the forest speaks,
Of hidden paths and mystic peaks.
Glimmers of wonder take their flight,
In pines embraced by soft moonlight.

The Enchantment of Colorful Currents

By the river where colors meet,
Waves dance with a rhythm sweet.
Currents sparkle, bright and clear,
Nature's magic, ever near.

Whirling eddies sing their song,
In this space, we all belong.
Reflections of the azure sky,
Dreamlike visions flutter by.

Pebbles glisten, smooth and round,
Holding treasures from the ground.
Ripples whisper soft and low,
Secrets meant for hearts to know.

Dancing leaves upon the shore,
Invite us in to explore.
Beneath the surface, life abounds,
In this enchantment, joy resounds.

As daylight fades, the stars awake,
In the stillness, dreams we make.
The currents sing their lullabies,
A vibrant world beneath the skies.

Splashes of Joy in the Sun-Dappled Glade

In the glade where laughter flows,
Sunshine warms the earth that grows.
Wildflowers burst in vibrant hue,
Their bright faces greet the view.

Children chase the shimmering light,
Through the meadows, pure delight.
With each step, the world awakes,
A tapestry the spirit makes.

Golden rays through leaves cascade,
In this sacred, joyous glade.
All around, a symphony,
Nature's song, our harmony.

Butterflies twirl and sway,
Painting magic in the day.
Every corner sings a tune,
Underneath the brightened moon.

As shadows stretch and daylight fades,
Joy lingers in the glade.
With splashes of color, life renews,
In every heart, the wonder brews.

Nature's Brushstrokes in a Sunlit World

Gentle rays dance through the trees,
Each leaf a canvas, each shadow a tease.
Bright flowers unfold, a vibrant embrace,
Nature's palette paints every space.

Whispers of wind in the morning dew,
A chorus of colors, fresh and true.
Golden beams sparkle on rippling streams,
In this sunlit world, we find our dreams.

Mountains stand tall, their peaks crowned with snow,
While valleys below in lush gardens grow.
Clouds drift softly, like thoughts in the mind,
In nature's brushstrokes, pure peace we find.

Painted horizons where sun meets the sea,
Each sunset a symphony, wild and free.
Life thrives in this ever-changing scene,
Nature's brushstrokes, a visual dream.

As twilight descends, stars softly gleam,
Each twinkle a whisper, a silent theme.
In nature's embrace, we silently stand,
Before this masterpiece, hand in hand.

The Colorful Harmony of a Hidden Spring

In secret glades where soft waters flow,
Petals awaken, put on their show.
Butterflies flit on delicate wings,
In this hidden spring, pure joy it brings.

A tapestry woven of green and gold,
Whispers of stories from times untold.
Among ancient trees, where shadows play,
Life finds a rhythm in nature's ballet.

Crimson blooms dance with lavender's grace,
In the sunlit embrace of a tranquil place.
Every drop glistens, each leaf sings its part,
In the colorful harmony, I find my heart.

Ripples of laughter in the gentle breeze,
Nature's sweet song putting minds at ease.
Cascading whispers of soft, flowing streams,
Here in the spring, we weave our dreams.

As dusk wraps the world in a velvety shroud,
A symphony of colors, vibrant and loud.
In this hidden place, all worries take wing,
In the colorful harmony of a hidden spring.

Beyond the Boughs: A Colorful Reverie

Beyond the boughs, where light filters through,
A realm full of wonder, painted anew.
Whispers of secrets on every soft breeze,
In moments like these, our spirits find ease.

Golden sunbeams break through the trees,
Painting shadows that dance with the leaves.
In a vibrant world where hope intertwines,
Every petal and leaf tells stories divine.

Frogs croak in harmony by the cool stream's edge,
While dragonflies dart, their bright colors pledge.
Crisp autumn winds weave a tale through the air,
In this colorful reverie, worries seem rare.

Birds serenade the twilight hour,
With melodies sweet, nature's power.
Each moment a glimpse of life's perfect grace,
Beyond the boughs, we find our place.

Starlight peeks shyly through branches above,
In a cosmos of dreams, we feel our love.
Beyond the boughs, in this magical throng,
We dance to the rhythm of nature's sweet song.

The Glossy Carrots of Wild Ferns

Deep in the woods where wild ferns grow,
The glossy carrots quietly glow.
Nurtured by shadows, kissed by the rain,
In the forest's embrace, they thrive without pain.

Emerald fronds dance with grace in the breeze,
Whispering secrets to thickets and trees.
With a splash of orange, life bursts forth,
The glossy carrots proclaim their worth.

In patches of sunlight that flicker and sway,
Nature reveals her bounty each day.
A hidden treasure, a vibrant delight,
These carrots of wild ferns, a colorful sight.

Amidst the soft rustle of leaves overhead,
A world of wonder where all dreams thread.
Where colors unite in a playful dance,
In nature's canvas, we find our chance.

As twilight descends and shadows grow long,
The forest hums gently a mystical song.
In the heart of the woods, we watch and we yearn,
For the glossy carrots of wild ferns.

Whispers Through Colorful Canopies

Leaves rustle softly in the breeze,
A symphony of whispers among the trees.
Colors dance gently, a vibrant show,
Where sunlight filters, painting the flow.

Birds sing sweetly, their melodies rise,
Echoing softly beneath painted skies.
Each hue tells a story, each shadow a tale,
In this wondrous haven where dreams set sail.

Nature's embrace wraps around my heart,
In this canvas of life, where all play a part.
The whispers of color, a soothing balm,
In this forest of wonder, I find my calm.

Sunlight fades slowly, a golden hue,
As twilight descends, painting the view.
With each passing moment, the colors play,
A vivid reminder of life's rich array.

Under the branches, my spirit takes flight,
In whispers of color, I find my light.
This sanctuary of nature, forever I'll roam,
In the arms of the forest, I feel at home.

Dappled Light Beneath the Emerald Canopy

Sunlight filters through, a gentle stream,
Casting soft patterns that weave like a dream.
Footsteps are quiet on the soft, cool ground,
In this emerald haven, peace can be found.

The air is fragrant with earth and with pine,
Each breath I take feels sacred, divine.
Flickers of gold dance on leaves so bright,
Under the canopy, all feels right.

Moss cushions my path, a velvety carpet,
Here in the stillness, my worries depart.
Nature's embrace wraps around me tight,
In dappled light, everything feels right.

The chorus of silence sings sweetly to me,
In the heart of the woods, I'm wild and I'm free.
Golden beams breaking through emerald green,
A moment of magic, serene and unseen.

As shadows grow longer, the day starts to fade,
Each dappled light whisper, a promise made.
In the emerald canopy, my spirit will stay,
Forever enchanted, in nature's ballet.

Reflections in the Crystal Waters

The lake lies still, a mirror so clear,
Reflecting the world that feels so near.
Mountains encircle, majestic and bold,
In nature's embrace, a story unfolds.

Ripples arise with a gentle breeze,
Dancing on waters, like whispers of trees.
Each reflection tells of moments gone by,
In this tranquil realm where the heart can fly.

Clouds drift softly, casting shadows below,
With every movement, the waters will flow.
Colors shimmer, a rainbow array,
In the crystal waters, life finds its way.

The sun dips low, painting skies aflame,
Each hue in the waters calls out a name.
With every sunset, the magic will stay,
In reflections of beauty, come what may.

The stillness lingers, a moment divine,
In the crystal waters, my spirit entwines.
Nature's embrace, a serene lullaby,
Reflecting the beauty of earth and sky.

The Dance of Hues in Woodland Streams

Beneath the trees, where sunlight beams,
Color flows freely in woodland streams.
Each ripple and wave, in motion so bright,
A dance of hues in the soft morning light.

Smooth stones glisten, their colors revealed,
In this vibrant tapestry, nature's field.
The water rushes, a joyful refrain,
Singing of life in the gentle terrain.

Leaves flutter softly, dropping down low,
Brushes of colors in the bubbly flow.
Crimson and gold intermingle with green,
In the dance of the water, a sight to be seen.

As I wander close, the cool waters greet,
Inviting my spirit, light, and discreet.
In the woodland's embrace, I'm lost in the dream,
Where nature's palette flows free in the stream.

Evening descends on this magical place,
The last hues of daylight softening their grace.
With every reflection, a promise bestowed,
In the dance of hues, my heart finds its road.

Shimmering Tapestries of Nature's Palette

In the morning's gentle light,
Colors blend with pure delight.
Petals dance in softest breeze,
Nature weaves with grace and ease.

Golden hues and emerald greens,
Each shade tells of quiet dreams.
Rivers shimmer, skies unfold,
Stories whispered, tales retold.

Birds in flight, a vivid show,
Dancing patterns, high and low.
Leaves like jewels in sunlight's kiss,
Every moment pure bliss.

The sunset paints with strokes of fire,
Capturing all that we desire.
The horizon glows, a canvas bright,
A fleeting glimpse of day and night.

In every crack, in every seam,
Nature's art fuels every dream.
A tapestry forever sewn,
In every heart, it is known.

Beneath the Luminous Treetops

Trees like giants touch the sky,
Whispers float as breezes sigh.
Roots embrace the earth so deep,
Where secrets of the wild do sleep.

Sunlight filters through the leaves,
Casting shadows, nature weaves.
A symphony of sounds all around,
In every rustle, magic found.

Birds chirp softly up above,
Echoing the songs of love.
Ferns unfurl, the ground so green,
In this realm, we're never seen.

Mossy carpets, soft and lush,
In the quiet, feel the hush.
Life intertwines, intricate dance,
Beneath the trees, we find our chance.

Each step taken is a prayer,
To the beauty that we share.
Beneath the luminous treetops high,
We breathe, we dream, we learn to fly.

Vibrations of Light in a Serene Landscape

Awake in dawn's soft embrace,
Whispers echo, nature's grace.
Mountains rise in misty veils,
Every corner, a story trails.

Fields of gold stretch far and wide,
Gentle waves like the ocean's tide.
Colors shift with the warming sun,
Every moment, a gift begun.

Clouds drift lazily in a stream,
Reflecting the sky's vibrant dream.
Ripples dance on the surface clear,
In this space, we shed our fear.

Trees stand tall, stoic and wise,
Guardians beneath the vast skies.
Vibrations of light, soft and bright,
Feed the heart with pure delight.

In this landscape, peace abounds,
In the silence, life resounds.
A canvas of dreams, a sacred land,
Where heart and soul go hand in hand.

Hidden Wonders of the Colorful Dell

In a dell where secrets lay,
Colors burst in wild array.
Flowers bloom with fragrant sighs,
Underneath the vast, blue skies.

Streams weave gently, crystal clear,
Mirroring the world we hold dear.
Butterflies flutter, spirits bright,
Painting moments with their flight.

Whispers of the wind take flight,
Carrying tales from day to night.
Beneath the boughs, treasures found,
In this haven, love surrounds.

The call of the meadowlark sings,
Nature's chorus, joy it brings.
Each corner holds a tale to tell,
In the heart of the colorful dell.

Beneath each blossom, magic flows,
In a world where beauty grows.
Hidden wonders wait to see,
In this dell, wild and free.

The Singing Brook and its Spectrum of Light

The brook flows softly, a gentle sound,
Reflecting colors, dancing all around.
Sunlight dapples on the water's face,
A tranquil melody, a sweet embrace.

Ripples shimmer with the hues of gold,
A fleeting story waiting to be told.
Nature's laughter echoes through the stream,
In every note, a dream within a dream.

Leaves whisper secrets to the rushing tide,
As sunlight weaves through branches side by side.
The world at play in a sparkling show,
In the singing brook, where wonders flow.

Fish dart swiftly, glimmers on their scale,
While dragonflies flit, their gossamer trail.
Colors collide in a joyful spree,
In this sacred space, where hearts wander free.

At dusk, the brook sings a lullaby,
Under the stars, where memories lie.
The spectrum of light fades into night,
But the song lingers, a soothing light.

Nature's Whisper in the Prism of Leaves

Among the branches, whispers glide,
In each rustling leaf, secrets abide.
The sun breaks through in a golden hue,
Crafting shadows that slip and renew.

A chorus of colors, vibrant and bright,
Nature's palette in the soft twilight.
Emerald greens and amber tones,
In every rustle, the forest moans.

Petals flutter like a painter's brush,
Creating art in the evening hush.
Their gentle beauty, a sight so rare,
Nature's marvel suspended in air.

Softly the wind sings through the trees,
A delicate dance, a gentle breeze.
Each color a note, in a symphonic play,
Nature's whisper guides the day away.

As dusk descends with a tender sigh,
The colors fade to a starlit sky.
Yet in the dark, new dreams take flight,
In the prism of leaves, a world of light.

Harmonies of Color Under the Vaulted Canopy

Under the canopy, colors entwine,
Creating harmonies, a sight divine.
With each passing breeze, a flutter, a sigh,
Nature's orchestra beneath the sky.

The blush of dawn spills its rosy glow,
Illuminating petals that dance below.
Golden yellows stretch towards the sun,
In this kaleidoscope, life has begun.

Branches reach out, a protective dome,
Cradling the earth, making it a home.
Every rustle tells a tale untold,
In whispers of green and vibrant gold.

The melody of life begins to swell,
Every note a story, every sound a spell.
Amidst the leaves, the colors engage,
Crafting a symphony upon nature's stage.

As twilight descends, colors fade to gray,
Yet the harmonies linger, they wish to stay.
In every heartbeat, nature sings bright,
Under the vaulted canopy, pure delight.

Sunlit Dreams in the Gnome Forest

In the gnome forest, dreams dance in light,
Sunbeams thread through the leaves, so bright.
Whispers of magic on the soft breeze,
Where time stands still, and worries freeze.

Mushrooms pop up in a playful array,
Tiny homes where the gnomes come to play.
Colors sparkling like gems on the ground,
In this hidden realm, joy can be found.

The song of the brook is a gentle hum,
A melody sweet, inviting all to come.
Each step on the moss, a soft little tune,
Under the watchful gaze of the moon.

Sunlit dreams weave stories untold,
In every shadow, adventures unfold.
In the heart of the woods, life flows serene,
In the gnome forest, a fairy tale scene.

As daylight wanes, the fireflies gleam,
Lighting the path towards each little dream.
In this sacred space, peace is our guide,
In the gnome forest, where love will abide.

The Palette of the Whispering Woods

In the woods where shadows play,
Colors softly blend and sway,
Leaves of gold and emerald bright,
Dance together in the light.

Whispers float on the gentle breeze,
Painting secrets among the trees,
Rustling sounds in harmony,
Nature's brush sets colors free.

Birdsongs echo, sweet and clear,
Melodies for all to hear,
Each note a stroke, a vibrant hue,
Crafting worlds both old and new.

Sunlight dapples, soft and warm,
Transforming all with gentle charm,
Mossy greens and earthy browns,
Stitch a quilt as nature crowns.

In every corner, art unfolds,
A canvas rich with stories told,
From the roots up to the sky,
In whispered woods, colors fly.

Glimmers at the Brook's Edge

Where the brook meets waters clear,
Glimmers dance, the scene is dear,
Sunlight sparkles, diamonds thrown,
On the surface, secrets shown.

Ribbons of blue, a silver thread,
Gentle currents softly spread,
Whispers murmur, tales of old,
Underneath the shadows bold.

Pebbles glisten, nature's gems,
Amidst the rush, a tranquil hymn,
Dragonflies dart, a fleeting sight,
Painting joy in pure delight.

Skimming stones, a child at play,
Ripples, laughter, bright as day,
Each splash a memory that sings,
Of summer warmth and joyous things.

As the twilight bids farewell,
Colors blend, and time will tell,
The brook keeps flowing, ever true,
In each glimmer, life renews.

Harmonies of Hues Amidst the Ferns

In the glen where ferns abound,
Harmonies of hues resound,
Emerald fronds in chorus sway,
Melodies of night and day.

Sunbeams filter, warm and bright,
Kissing petals, soft daylight,
Colors mingle, a vibrant throng,
Nature's pulse, a timeless song.

Crisp air whispers through the leaves,
As the heart of nature breathes,
Palette rich with life anew,
From the earth, each shade imbues.

Textures weave a tapestry,
Calling forth a symphony,
Shadows dance in leafy grace,
Painting joy in this sacred space.

In the hush where stillness reigns,
Life's sweet magic gently gains,
Harmony in every tone,
In the ferns, we find our home.

Secrets of the Chromatic Glade

In the glade where colors bloom,
Secrets linger, soft as gloom,
Petals whisper tales untold,
In vibrant strokes, a dream unfolds.

Rays of sun break through the leaves,
Caressing hues, the earth believes,
Every shade has a story clear,
In the glade, all hearts draw near.

Crimson, azure, and gold entwine,
A palette rich, by design,
Fluttering wings, a fleeting sight,
Adding joy to the soft light.

Breezes carry scents so sweet,
Every step feels like a treat,
Nature's brush, with colors bold,
Unveils the life that it holds.

Time stands still where beauty grows,
In the glade, true magic flows,
Secrets shared in petals' grace,
In chromatic dreams, we embrace.

Fables of the Glistening Glade

In the glade where whispers play,
Stories told in the light of day,
Mossy stones and flowers bright,
Nature dances, pure delight.

Breezes carry tales so old,
Of the brave and the bold,
Underneath the ancient trees,
Secrets shared with every breeze.

Twinkling stars in evening's grace,
Guide the hearts that seek this place,
Moonlit paths where shadows creep,
In the glade, our dreams we keep.

Creatures watch with knowing eyes,
As the night begins to rise,
Fables woven in the night,
In the glade, all is right.

When dawn breaks with golden hue,
Life awakens fresh and new,
Echoing the tales of yore,
In the glade forevermore.

Reflections in a Spectrum of Dappled Light

Shafts of sun through leaves do weave,
Patterns soft, they dance and cleave,
Colors burst in gentle rays,
Nature's palette sings and plays.

Rippling streams, they shimmer still,
Mirroring the dreams we fill,
In the glen where light does fall,
We find hope and love for all.

Petals flutter, vibrant hues,
Whispers of the morning's views,
Within shadows, spirits glide,
In this canvas, we abide.

Birds at dawn begin to sing,
Melodies on soft winds swing,
Through the trees, their voices rise,
Echoing through azure skies.

In this space of light and shade,
Infinite stories have been made,
Reflections caught in nature's art,
In every hue, a beating heart.

Chasing Rainbows Through the Misty Vale

In the vale where colors blend,
Chasing rainbows, dreams ascend,
Mist enfolds the softest light,
Whispers weave the day to night.

Footsteps dance on emerald grass,
Through the fog, the visions pass,
Hues of joy, they sparkle bright,
Glimmers of the purest light.

With each bend, the magic grows,
In the vale where laughter flows,
Chasing shadows, finding grace,
Every moment holds a trace.

Clouds drift by in soft embrace,
Carrying the dreams we chase,
Through the mist, we find our way,
To the dawn of a new day.

In the embrace of this wild sphere,
Hope arises, crystal clear,
Chasing dreams that never pale,
Together in the misty vale.

A Tapestry Woven with Radiance

Threads of gold in sunlight's weave,
Nature's gifts for all to grieve,
Embroidered tales of earth and sky,
Woven where our spirits fly.

In the fabric of the day,
Colors burst and dance and sway,
Each moment stitched with care,
In the tapestry we share.

Crimson leaves and sapphire streams,
Woven tightly into dreams,
Every stitch a story told,
In this vibrant quilt of gold.

Embrace the weft, embrace the warp,
Feel the rhythm, hear the harp,
Nature sings in every thread,
In this art, our hearts are led.

Through each line, our souls entwine,
In this tapestry, we shine,
Woven with love, radiant grace,
Together in this sacred space.

Shimmering Hues in the Twilit Thicket

In emerald glades where shadows play,
The sun dips low at end of day.
Crimson leaves in whispers sway,
While twilight weaves night's soft array.

A breeze carries scents of pine,
As silver stars begin to shine.
A world awake, serene, divine,
In hushed tones, nature's voice align.

Mossy carpets spread their touch,
Soft as dreams, yet firm as such.
In this realm, we feel so much,
The heart's pulse is a gentle clutch.

Golden shafts of light break through,
Painting all in soft pastels hue.
Where woodland secrets twirl anew,
In the thicket, life's whispers grew.

As night engulfs the fading light,
The magic sparkles, pure delight.
In shimmering hues, a soft sight,
Guiding dreams till morning's bright.

Radiant Echoes by the Woodland Spring

Near the brook where wildflowers bloom,
Echoes dance, dispelling gloom.
Sunlight filters, weaving room,
In this place where hearts assume.

Rippling waters, clear and bright,
Reflecting visions, purest light.
Nature's canvas, a wondrous sight,
Filling souls with sheer delight.

Whispers swirl beneath the trees,
Carried softly by the breeze.
Every note, a gentle tease,
In this harmony, we find ease.

Butterflies in colors bold,
Stories of the woods unfold.
In the shadows, tales retold,
Radiant echoes, dreams of gold.

As sunset fades, the colors blend,
A symphony that seems to mend.
By the spring where hearts transcend,
Eternal moments never end.

Chromatic Ripples at Dusk's Embrace

At dusk's embrace, the colors swirl,
Each hue a story, thoughts unfurl.
Glossy lakes in twilight twirl,
Nature's charm begins to whirl.

Crimson skies and indigo seas,
Stretched between the whispering trees.
In calm repose, the spirit frees,
In chromatic waves, a gentle ease.

The moon climbs high, the stars ignite,
Painting dreams with purest light.
In quietude, the world feels right,
As ripples dance in fading sight.

Nature's palette does not tire,
With every brushstroke, hearts inspire.
Fueling our dreams, kindling fire,
In twilight's glow, we never tire.

When dawn approaches, hues will sway,
Carving paths for the day's ballet.
Yet in this twilight, joy will stay,
In chromatic ripples, come what may.

The Gnome's Secret Garden of Illumination

In hidden glens where gnomes reside,
A garden blooms with joy and pride.
Flickering lights as fairies glide,
In secret realms, magic won't hide.

Petals painted with the sun,
Laughter echoes, a joyful run.
In every corner, life's begun,
Embraced by warmth, we come as one.

Mushroom rings and willows sway,
Beneath the stars that softly play.
In this gilded, secret way,
Illumination leads the way.

Whimsical paths with scents that tease,
Winding deep through ancient trees.
Where every breath feels like a breeze,
In gnome's dance, the heart finds ease.

Here in the night, we rest our heads,
On soft moss beds, where kindness spreads.
In the garden where magic treads,
Illuminate the dreams it sheds.

Celestial Simmering Over Mossy Stones

Stars dance softly on the brook,
Whispers weave through ancient nooks,
Moonlight ripples, silver streams,
Nature hums in dreamy themes.

Mossy stones in twilight's glow,
Crickets sing as breezes flow,
Each moment wrapped in misty veils,
The night's embrace, a tale that trails.

Reflections shimmer, hearts ignite,
Within the dark, a spark of light,
Time meanders, slow and free,
In this realm, just you and me.

The air is thick with magic's hue,
As shadows play with the night's dew,
Every breath a whispered prayer,
Celestial moments linger in the air.

Underneath a starlit dome,
Here in nature, we feel at home,
With every stone and every stream,
We find the essence of our dream.

Vibrant Vistas Where Myth Meets Light

On distant hills, the sun awakes,
Painting skies with golden flakes,
Legends rise from fiery hues,
As dawn ignites the waking muse.

Fields of lavender softly sway,
Where whispers from the myths hold sway,
Heroes dance in shafts of sun,
In vibrant tales, our hearts are spun.

Every shadow tells a tale,
Of love, of loss, a timeless trail,
In the embrace of nature's sight,
We glimpse the truth beyond the light.

Echoes call through valleys deep,
Where ancient secrets yearn to leap,
In the harmony of day and night,
Myth and reality merge in flight.

Beneath the vast, embracing skies,
We seek the wondrous, seek the wise,
In every vista, dreams take flight,
As vibrant worlds unfold in light.

The Hidden Prism Beneath the Leaves

Beneath the canopy of green,
A world of colors yet unseen,
Light refracts through leafy lace,
Revealing magic in this space.

Each step reveals a vibrant glow,
Shadows dance, ebb and flow,
Flecks of gold and shades of blue,
The whispers of the forest crew.

In this silence, secrets tease,
Echoes drift on gentle breeze,
Every leaf a story spun,
In tangled roots, the tales begun.

Nature's heart beats loud and clear,
In hidden prisms, we draw near,
With every glance, we find the core,
Of life's vast beauty, evermore.

Beneath the boughs, we softly tread,
Where colors merge, and doubts are shed,
In this sanctuary, we believe,
In the power of what we perceive.

Enigmatic Colors in the Silhouette of Trees

Twilight wraps the world in gray,
Where trees stand tall, shadows play,
Enigmatic forms reach high,
Against the canvas of the sky.

Whispers come from every leaf,
In the dusk, a sigh of grief,
Vivid hues begin to gleam,
Painting nature's hidden dream.

In the stillness, secrets bloom,
As night enfolds, dispelling gloom,
With every branch, the stories weave,
In the silhouettes, we believe.

Crimson shades and indigo,
Flow like rivers, soft and slow,
In the night's embrace, we see
The colors dance, wild and free.

As dawn approaches, hues dissolve,
Yet in our hearts, they still revolve,
In every tree, a tale to share,
Of enigmatic colors in the air.

The Fusion of Nature's Palette with Dawn's Awakening

Crimson hues kiss the waking sky,
Whispers of light begin to sigh.
Golden rays dance on dew-kissed leaves,
Nature's song, as the world believes.

Trees stand tall, silhouetted bright,
Awakening hearts with morning light.
Birds chirp softly, a sweet refrain,
Crafting harmony in the gentle rain.

Clouds brush across the azure dome,
In this embrace, the wild finds home.
Sunbeams twinkle through bright green crowns,
As dawn unravels her vibrant gowns.

Colors blend in a soft caress,
Morning's canvas, nature's dress.
Each brushstroke tells a tale anew,
Of life reborn, with each sun's view.

The air, a mosaic of scents divine,
Fills the spirit with warmth, a sign.
Nature awakened, a splendid show,
A fusion of beauty, forever to grow.

Serenade of Colors in the Gentle Breeze

In fields where wildflowers bloom bright,
Colors whisper in the soft twilight.
Dancing petals in a gentle sway,
Nature's ballet at the end of day.

Lavender sighs in aromatic bliss,
While golden sunbeams weave through the kiss.
The breeze carries stories of the land,
A serenade crafted by nature's hand.

Blue above, with clouds soft and white,
Glimmers of stars begin their flight.
In the dusk, colors intertwine,
As night drapes the world in designs divine.

Each hue sings of a tranquil place,
A tapestry woven with perfect grace.
The gentle wind, a playful muse,
In this colorful world, we all choose.

Moments painted with strokes of fate,
Nature's palette, a scene so great.
In gentle breezes, life shall sway,
A serenade that will not fray.

Embrace of the Vibrant Woodlands

In the woodlands where giants stand tall,
Nature calls softly, inviting all.
Leafy canopies, a verdant dream,
In shadows and light, the echoes scream.

Moss carpets cradle the ancient ground,
In the stillness, whispers abound.
Wild creatures dance through emerald trails,
Their laughter ringing, as life prevails.

Sunlight filters with fragments of gold,
Stories of nature quietly told.
Each rustling leaf sings a gentle tune,
In the embrace of the dappled moon.

Winds weave through branches, a sweet embrace,
In vibrant hues, find a tranquil space.
Woodlands pulse with life, under skies,
With every heartbeat, a new surprise.

Nature's canvas, rich and profound,
In vibrant woodlands, magic is found.
An eternal cycle, strong and free,
In this embrace, simply to be.

Moments of Radiance in Silent Glades

In silent glades where secrets sleep,
Moments of magic softly seep.
Radiance spills from sunlit streams,
Awakening hearts, igniting dreams.

A carpet of leaves in hues of brown,
Crimson and amber gently lay down.
In tranquil stillness, time stands still,
Nature whispers, an echoing thrill.

Delicate ferns in soft embrace,
Catch the light, each shape finds its place.
Butterflies flit in kaleidoscope trails,
Painting the air with their delicate sails.

In every shadow, a flicker of grace,
Moments held tight in this sacred space.
The chirp of crickets, a rhythmic guide,
In silent glades, dreams abide.

The quiet rustle of the gentle trees,
A melody carried on the breeze.
In these moments where life unravels,
Radiance blooms, as the heart travels.